AUGUSTUS
and Imperial Rome

by Miriam Greenblatt

BENCHMARK BOOKS

MARSHALL CAVENDISH
NEW YORK

ACKNOWLEDGMENT

With thanks to Sara Phang, doctoral candidate in the
Department of History, Columbia University, New York City,
for her assistance in preparing the manuscript.

Benchmark Books
Marshall Cavendish Corporation
99 White Plains Road
Tarrytown, New York 10591
Copyright © 2000 by Marshall Cavendish Corporation

Library of Congress Cataloging-in-Publication Data
Greenblatt, Miriam.
Augustus and Imperial Rome / by Miriam Greenblatt.
p.   cm.—(Rulers and their times)
Includes bibliographical references and index.
Summary: Examines the rule of Augustus Caesar, including his rise to power,
politics, and final days, and describes everyday life in Rome during his reign.
ISBN 0-7614-0912-2
1. Augustus, Emperor of Rome, 63 B.C.-14 A.D.—Juvenile literature.
2. Emperors—Rome—Biography—Juvenile literature. 3. Rome—Social life
and customs—Juvenile literature. [1. Augustus, Emperor of Rome, 63 B.C.–14 A.D.
2. Kings, queens, rulers, etc. 3. Rome—Civilization.] I. Title II. Series.
DG279.G73   1999   937′.07′092—dc21   [B]   98-25654   CIP   AC

Printed in Hong Kong
1   3   5   6   4   2

Picture research by Linda Sykes, Hilton Head, SC

Cover: Bridgeman Art Library; page 5: Vatican Museum/Scala/Art Resource; pages 6–7: Palazzo
Madama, Rome/Scala/Art Resource; page 9: Rheinisches, Landesmuseum, Trier/Erich Lessing/Art
Resource; page 12: Museo Nazionale Romano, Rome/Erich Lessing/Art Resource; pages 19, 31:
Bridgeman Art Library; page 23: Palazzo dei Conservatori, Rome/Nimatallah/Art Resource; page 24:
Kunsthistoriches, Vienna/Bridgeman Art Library; pages 26–27: Bardo Museum/Gilles Mermet/AKG,
London; pages 29, 50: Scala/Art Resource; pages 34, 37: AKG, London; page 40: The Metropolitan
Museum of Art, Rogers Fund, 1903; pages 42, 65: Erich Lessing/Art Resource; page 44: Superstock;
page 45 (right): Borghese Gallery, Rome/Scala/Art Resource; page 45 (left): Museo Archaeologico,
Naples/e.t.archive; page 47: Museo Archaeologico, Naples/Erich Lessing/Art Resource; page 56:
Rheinisches Landesmuseum, Trier/Erich Lessing/Art Resource; page 57: AKG/Superstock; pages
62–63: Museo Archaeologico Nazionale, Naples/Scala/Art Resource; page 68: Museo Prenestino
Palestrina, Rome/e.t.archive; page 71: Musée des Beaux-Arts André Malraux, Le Havre,
France/Giraudon/Art Resource

Contents

Rome's First Emperor

More than two thousand years ago, Rome was the largest city in the world. Its empire stretched from the Atlantic Ocean to the Persian Gulf and from the North Sea to the banks of the Nile. Millions of people spoke the Latin language, walked on Roman roads, and copied Roman architecture.

Yet Rome was also a city torn by civil wars that went on and on for about a hundred years. Many Romans despaired of the future. Then, in 31 B.C.E.,* Augustus put an end to the wars and shortly after became Rome's first emperor. The government he established gave the Mediterranean world two centuries of peace and prosperity and laid the foundation for modern Europe.

In this book, you will read how Augustus rose to power and how he reformed Rome. You will learn about the life of a soldier and that of a schoolboy, about the clothes the Romans wore, the foods they ate, the religions they followed, and the bloody entertainment they enjoyed. Finally, letters, poems, histories, and tombstone inscriptions will reveal what Romans themselves had to say about their city, its politics, and the Age of Augustus.

---

*Many systems of dating have been used by different cultures throughout history. This series of books uses B.C.E. (Before Common Era) and C.E. (Common Era) instead of B.C. (Before Christ) and A.D. (Anno Domini) out of respect for the diversity of the world's peoples.

Like George Washington,
Augustus is known as the
Father of His Country.

PART ONE

The Most

Although the Roman Senate opposed Augustus at first, it soon became a staunch supporter of the emperor.

Remarkable Roman

Early Years

Legends about people usually spring up after their death. In the case of Augustus, however, Romans were telling wondrous tales about him while he was still alive. They said his real father was the sun god Apollo, who had visited his mother in the shape of a snake. They said that one day when Augustus was a child, an eagle swooped out of the sky and snatched a crust of bread from his hands, only to return it uneaten. One Roman senator dreamed that a gold chain had lowered Augustus from heaven. Another dreamed that the supreme god Jupiter, father of the Roman state, had placed an image of the city in Augustus's lap. To Rome's inhabitants, Augustus was the most remarkable Roman who ever lived.

Augustus was born Gaius Octavius Thurinus in 63 B.C.E. Historians refer to him during this period as Octavian. His father died when he was a child and he was brought up by his mother, who later remarried.

When he was in his midteens, Octavian attracted the attention of his granduncle Julius Caesar. Caesar was impressed by Octavian's character. The youth was serious, studious, ambitious, and decisive. His appearance was good, too. He had curly blond hair, large gray eyes, and a pleasant voice. His only flaw was poor health. Although he ate little and drank less, his stomach was always getting upset. He suffered from liver abscesses and kidney stones, and he sometimes limped on his left leg. Despite these problems, he was quite vain. He shaved every day, unlike most Roman men, and wore shoes with built-up soles to make him look taller than he was.

For most of his teens, Octavian lived the life of a typical Roman aristocrat. In the morning, he studied Greek literature, philosophy, and public speaking to prepare for a career in government. He attended the law courts, where the Romans were always suing one another. In the afternoon, he played ball, lifted weights, and wrestled before having a bath and a massage. And in the evening, he attended dinner parties with his friends. Octavian also put in a tour of military service with his granduncle in Spain.

Then came the Ides of March, March 15, 44 B.C.E., and Octavian's life changed completely.

A teacher scolds a pupil for coming late to class. Writing was very important in the Roman world. Magistrates kept records of judgments, business people kept bills of sale and contracts, and families kept books containing prayers, medical remedies, and tips on farming.

A Political Crisis

To understand what happened to Octavian, it helps to know something about Rome's early history. The city was supposedly founded in 753 B.C.E., or the year 1 of the Roman calendar. Most archaeologists, however, believe Rome began as a small village around 1000 B.C.E. At first, the city was ruled by a king, but in 509 B.C.E. the Romans revolted and replaced the monarchy with a republic.

In the second century B.C.E., a number of civil wars broke out in the Roman Republic. On one side was the ruling Senate, which was made up mostly of landowning aristocrats. On the other side were a series of political reformers and military strongmen. The reformers thought the government had become corrupt and was ignoring the welfare of the average Roman. They wanted to take over the public land the rich had grabbed for themselves and distribute it to unemployed citizens. The military strongmen were ambitious and wanted power for themselves. Also, they realized that the Senate was unable to govern the empire effectively.

In 46 B.C.E., the military leader Julius Caesar became dictator, or absolute ruler, of Rome. Once in office, he tried to improve the lot of his landless soldiers, who had helped him come to power. He resettled 80,000 of them in overseas colonies and hired additional thousands to build roads and improve harbors. He expanded Roman citizenship to include the Spaniards, Gauls, and Greeks who had supported him. He also tried to cut down the power of the Senate, whose members usually served for life. He increased its numbers with his own appointees, mostly bankers, merchants, and manufacturers.

Needless to say, the landowning aristocrats resented Caesar tremendously. They were convinced he planned to abolish the Roman Republic and set himself up as a divine monarch. After all, didn't he wear purple robes—the color of royalty—in public? Hadn't he ordered a statue of himself placed among the statues of Rome's first seven kings, who had ruled the city more than four hundred years earlier? Most shocking of all was the rumor that he planned to marry his lover, Cleopatra, queen of Egypt, and move the empire's capital from Rome to Alexandria. Accordingly, some sixty senators organized a conspiracy, and on the Ides of March they stabbed Julius Caesar to death.

A few days later, Caesar's will was read. In it, he adopted Octavian as his son and left him three-fourths of his immense fortune. He also threw open his gardens along the Tiber River as a public park and promised every citizen a cash gift.

Caesar's will delighted the people of Rome. But it gravely disappointed Caesar's right-hand man, Mark Antony. Antony had fought side by side with the late dictator and then had helped him govern. He had delivered such a stirring funeral oration over Caesar's body that his listeners had driven the assassins out of the city. If anyone should be Caesar's heir, thought Antony, it should be me, not a nineteen-year-old boy who has not even won a single battle.

When news of Caesar's will reached Octavian—who was then studying abroad—he determined to go to Rome at once. His

Civil wars had been disrupting the Roman state for more than a century before Augustus came to power.

mother and stepfather tried to dissuade him. He didn't need Caesar's money, they said; he would still be a rich man. Also, they pointed out, Antony had already seized partial control of Rome, as well as Caesar's treasure, and would certainly oppose him. The Senate, too, was bound to resent him. But Octavian paid no attention. He was determined both to avenge his granduncle's murder and to gain political power for himself.

As matters turned out, Octavian's family needn't have worried. The youth was a natural-born politician who knew exactly what to do.

Octavian began by adding Caesar's name to part of his. He became Gaius Julius Caesar Octavianus. The new name gave him prestige. Then, since Antony refused to release Caesar's treasure, Octavian borrowed all the money he could from his mother, stepfather, and two cousins and paid off Caesar's legacy to the people of Rome. That gave him popularity. Next, he organized an army of Caesar's veterans. That gave him a power base. Finally, he offered his services to the Senate in its political struggle with Antony.

The senators at first tried to make Octavian serve their own purposes. As one Senate leader wrote, "The young man should be flattered, used, and pushed aside." But the senators badly misjudged Octavian. After winning a victory against Antony only to be snubbed by the Senate, Octavian turned around and joined forces with his former enemy. The two men, together with Marcus Aemilius Lepidus, one of Caesar's generals, then formed what is known as the Second Triumvirate, or group of three rulers. They made plans to take over the Roman Empire.

The first item on their agenda was defeating the armies of Caesar's assassins. That meant the triumvirate needed money with which to pay their own troops. So they drew up a list of three hundred senators and two thousand members of the upper middle class, accused them of having taken part in Caesar's murder, and called on the Romans to punish them with death. Some of the accused *were* guilty, and all were political opponents of the triumvirate. But the main reason their names appeared on the death list was that they owned vast estates the triumvirs could confiscate.

For the next several weeks, terror reigned in Rome. The accused were murdered on the streets or slain in their beds. Every day, men carrying sacks full of heads claimed the promised reward: five hundred dollars per head if the killer was a freed man, two hundred dollars and freedom if he was a slave. The purge was unquestionably the worst act of Octavian's career.

When the killing was over, the triumvirs had enough money to pay their soldiers. They defeated the armies of Caesar's assassins, thus avenging the late dictator's death. Then they divided up the empire. Antony took charge of Gaul (present-day France) and the lands east of Italy. Octavian took charge of North Africa, the island of Sicily, and Spain. And the three rulers governed the Italian peninsula together.

Octavian versus Antony

For several years all went well. Then Lepidus, who was the weakest of the three, was forced to retire, and the rivalry between Octavian and Antony started up again. The rivalry was partly military, partly personal.

Octavian had been successful in the Mediterranean. He had safeguarded trade by wiping out the pirates who had been capturing Egyptian grain ships headed for Rome. In contrast, Antony had lost two separate campaigns against the Parthians in Persia.

Antony had personal problems as well. He had fallen in love with Queen Cleopatra of Egypt, Caesar's former lover. That would not have mattered except for the fact that he was already married to Octavian's sister, Octavia. Antony finally divorced Octavia and married Cleopatra, even though marrying a foreigner was contrary to Roman law. Octavian was furious at the insult to his family. He became even more furious when Antony announced that Cleopatra's son Caesarion was Julius Caesar's legitimate child. What Antony was really saying was that Octavian had no legal right to Caesar's name and inheritance; both belonged to Caesarion.

Yet the contest between Octavian and Antony was more than a personal struggle between two ambitious men. It was also a fight about the future of Rome. In a sense, Antony had turned his back on the city to live with Cleopatra in Egypt, a land most Romans considered corrupt, despotic, and superstitious. Octavian wanted to restore the old Roman virtues of good government and plain living.

The showdown between Octavian and Antony took place on September 3, 31 B.C.E., when their two fleets met near Actium, Greece. Antony's fleet was larger and more heavily armored. Yet Octavian won. Why? Because in the midst of the battle, the ship carrying Cleopatra began to sail away. And Antony, forgetting the thousands of men who were fighting for him, abandoned his fleet and his army and sailed after her. Two hours later, the battle of Actium was over.

The following summer, Octavian invaded Egypt and captured Alexandria. Antony and Cleopatra committed suicide, while Caesarion was executed. Octavian was now undisputed master of the Roman world.

Ruling Rome

As he had after the death of Julius Caesar, Octavian again proved to be a natural-born politician. He was convinced that Rome needed strong, one-man rule. But he realized that most Romans would go along only if they thought the Republic still existed. In other words, Octavian had to combine real power for himself with the appearance of power for the Senate.

Accordingly, Octavian rejected all titles such as king or emperor. "I refused every office which was contrary to the customs of our ancestors," he wrote later. The most he would agree to be called was Augustus, meaning "honored" or "revered one." He treated the Senate with great respect (although he weeded out several hundred senators who opposed him). He would rise from his seat whenever a senator entered the room. He always asked the Senate for advice (although he did not always take it). And he insisted that the Senate vote power to him for only a few years at a time. As a result, when he offered to give up his power in 27 B.C.E., the Senate not only refused his offer but voted to give him even more power.

Augustus's power was indeed immense. He controlled both the army and the government. Every soldier swore an oath of loyalty, not to Rome, but directly to Augustus. (To guarantee their loyalty, he gave the soldiers generous bonuses after major battles.) He had his own set of bureaucrats to help him administer the laws; they were the beginning of a true civil service.

Augustus was an excellent ruler. He organized a public police force and a public fire brigade to make Rome a safer place in which to live. He repaired and extended the aqueducts that supplied the city with water. He distributed free grain whenever there was a threat of famine. He carried out a massive building program that included new roads, theaters, law courts, and monuments. He once boasted that he had found Rome a city built of brick but was leaving it a city "clothed in marble."

As far as the empire was concerned, Augustus completed the conquest of Spain and pushed Rome's frontiers northward and eastward into the heart of Europe. He stationed soldiers permanently in frontier areas to keep out the Parthians, Germans, and other enemies. He strengthened Rome's relations with its provinces by promoting the religious cult of *Roma et Augustus*, "Rome and Augustus." People prayed for his good health and the empire's welfare at the same time. In Egypt and provinces to the east, where people believed their rulers were divine, Augustus was worshipped as a living god.

Augustus urged provincial governors to respect local customs so as to lessen the possibility of revolt. He had a census taken every fourteen years to make certain the land tax was fair. He set up a public postal service. And he resettled several hundred thousand unemployed army veterans in overseas colonies.

Augustus tried to inspire the Romans as well as rule them. He wanted them to be proud of their ancestry and their history. So he persuaded the poet Virgil to write an epic poem called the *Aeneid*. In his poem, Virgil told about the legendary adventures of the Trojan hero Aeneas, who was rescued by the gods after the Trojans were defeated by the Greeks. Aeneas eventually landed in Italy,

Public buildings throughout the Roman empire tended to be massive and imposing. This amphitheater is in Spain.

where his descendant Romulus founded Rome, naming the city after himself. The *Aeneid* did not glorify just Aeneas. It glorified all the Romans who helped turn a small village into a mighty empire. The *Aeneid* also emphasized Augustus's ideas about how to govern such an empire:

> Remember, Roman, to guide the nations with authority.
> Let these be your arts: to impose the habit of peace,
> To spare the humble and subdue the proud.

NORTH
SEA

BRITANNIA

Londinium
(London)

English Channel

ATLANTIC

OCEAN

Colonia Agrippina
(Cologne)

GERMANIA

Bonna
(Bonn)

GAUL

A L P S

HISPANIA

ADRIA

Rome

Misenum
Naples

Mou
Vesu

TYRRHENIAN
SEA

SICILY

Carthage

AFRICA

Extent of the Roman Empire

BLACK SEA

Danube River

Byzantium

ASIA MINOR

PARTHIA

Tigris River

MESOPOTAMIA

Troy

Pergamum

Euphrates River

Brundisium
(Brindisi)

MACEDONIA

Antioch

Actium

Athens

Damascus

Sparta

Tyre

JUDAEA

MEDITERRANEAN SEA

Jerusalem

Alexandria

N

EGYPT

Nile River

RED SEA

| 0 | 400 | 800 km |
| 0 | 250 | 500 mi |

Thebes

Livia Drusilla was intelligent as well as beautiful. She divorced her first husband in order to marry Augustus. As a member of the old-line aristocracy, she was a great political asset for the emperor.

But he needed a son to inherit the empire.

Augustus first adopted Marcellus, the son of his sister, Octavia. Marcellus, however, died in 23 B.C.E. Augustus then adopted Gaius and Lucius, his two grandsons. But they, too, died, Lucius in 2 C.E. from a fever and Gaius eighteen months later from a wound. With no male descendants of his own flesh and blood left to adopt, Augustus turned to his stepson Tiberius, Livia's son from her first marriage. Tiberius would be the second emperor of Rome.

By now, Augustus had been the first emperor—albeit without the title—for forty-four years. He had given the people peace and prosperity. He had ended the civil wars that had plagued Rome for years. He had reorganized the government and placed it on a firm footing. Foreign trade boomed as caravans brought in silk from China, spices from India, and amber, furs, and tin from northern Europe. Everyone used the same currency. Dozens of new cities sprang up. And Roman law extended over an empire of 50 to 70 million people. In later years when the Romans looked back at the reign of Augustus, they always called it the Golden Age.

The Final Days

The summer of 14 C.E. was extremely hot. Augustus was staying at his small country house near Naples. It was August, the month named after him. On August 19, the emperor woke up feeling very weak. It was hard for him to talk. He called for a mirror and ordered a servant to comb his hair. Livia and Tiberius, as well as some friends, were standing in his room. "How have I played my part in the comedy of life?" he asked. Then, trying to kiss his wife, he murmured, "Farewell, Livia, live mindful of our marriage" and died quickly and quietly.

The soldiers carrying Augustus's body back to Rome could travel only by night because of the heat. So the funeral did not take place until early September. A huge line of mourners, accompanied by trumpets and muffled drums, paraded through the city. The coffin was placed on a funeral pyre. Wine, oil, and spices were poured on top and then the pyre was set ablaze. As the flames rose, the watchers thought they saw an eagle come out of the smoke and ascend toward heaven. Surely it was Augustus going to his final resting place among the gods.

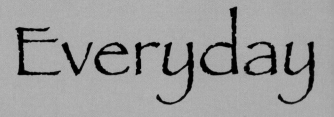

Everyday

PART TWO

A Roman farmer harvests olives. Olive oil was the most important commodity sold in Rome, where it was handled by more than two thousand dealers. The Romans used olive oil for cooking, in sauces and salad dressings, as a fuel for lamps, and for rubbing themselves after a bath.

Life in Imperial Rome

The Roman Legions

Rome lies about halfway down the west coast of Italy. The city was originally built on a group of seven hills along a bank of the Tiber River, fifteen miles inland from the Tyrrhenian Sea. The Tyrrhenian is an arm of the Mediterranean Sea. Romans of Augustus's time called the Mediterranean *mare nostrum*, "our sea," because Roman soldiers had extended the empire all around the Mediterranean's shores.

During Rome's early years, when it was still a republic, every male citizen served in the army, joining up whenever danger threatened. Under Augustus, the army became professional, and men enlisted for sixteen years (later, twenty years). The pay was quite small and had to cover both food and clothing. However, when a soldier retired, he received a discharge bonus of about ten to fourteen years' pay or a plot of land to farm. Also, whatever booty he obtained in war was his to keep. All this made the army a popular career choice.

Roman soldiers were known as legionaries because they were organized into legions of five thousand to six thousand men. Each legion had a number and a name. The name might refer to the place where the legion was formed or where it had once campaigned, or to a nickname it received in battle, or to the emperor who founded it. For example, Legio IX Hispana was the "ninth legion, raised in Spain," Legio XII Fulminata was the "twelfth

Rome and fighting seemed to go together. The Romans excelled at siege warfare and were also very skillful at maneuvering in the field.

legion, the Thunderbolts," and Legio III Augusta was the "third legion, founded by Augustus."

Every legion carried two standards, or sacred images, mounted on poles. One image was that of an imperial eagle, made of silver. It was inscribed with the letters *SPQR*, for *Senatus Populusque Romanus*, "the Senate and the people of Rome." The other image was the legion's special badge, often a totem animal such as a wolf or a boar. A legion that lost a standard was permanently disgraced.

When a legion went into battle, the youngest and least experienced soldiers would lead the attack. Older, more experienced soldiers followed, ready to relieve the front lines if necessary. And in the rear were the senior veterans, who would often split off from the main force and charge the enemy from the sides. This division of soldiers made a legion very flexible in battle. Moreover, because legionaries lined up at arm's length from one another, each was able to take on several opponents at the same time.

For long-distance fighting of eighty feet or more, a legionary carried two javelins to hurl at the enemy. On his right side hung a short double-edged iron sword with which to stab the enemy in close combat. His left hand held an iron-rimmed shield to protect his body. He also wore defensive armor consisting of an iron helmet and either a coat of mail or an iron-plated leather coat with a woolen tunic underneath. His sandals were made of leather studded with nails, and he put on a woolen cloak when the weather turned cold. Sometimes, if the weather was freezing, he wore "barbarian" trousers like those worn by the Germanic tribes of northern Europe.

Discipline in the Roman army involved both rewards and punishments. Rewards took two forms: promotion in rank and decorations. The decorations were usually made of gold and silver and were worn on the soldier's coat. Punishments depended on the offense. A soldier who committed a minor offense might be assigned extra watch duties or be served inferior food. If the offense was more serious, he might be fined or demoted. Cowards and deserters were punished by death. Sometimes an entire unit was decimated; that is, every tenth soldier was executed as a warning to the others.

Legionaries were highly trained. They made forced marches of twenty miles a day, every day, to build up their endurance. They spent long hours practicing the use of their swords. If there was water nearby, they learned to swim. Many developed specialized skills. They were surveyors, bridge builders, clerks, carpenters, masons, smiths, and artillerymen.

This Roman soldier carries a javelin and shield, and wears a coat of mail, iron helmet, and leather sandals.

They were also sometimes *muli Mariani,* or "Marius's mules." (Marius was a famous Roman general.) Usually each legion was accompanied by mules carrying grain and wine, as well as by ox-drawn carts containing leather tents, wooden stakes, tools, and cooking pots. Sometimes, though, a legion had to travel through heavily forested or mountainous country where mules and carts could not go. In such cases, the legionaries had no choice but to carry their supplies and gear themselves. Each legionary's burden generally weighed between forty and ninety pounds!

The legionaries used their trenching tools to build a fortified camp each night in which to sleep. They would level the ground if it was uneven, put up a wall with their wooden stakes, and surround the wall with a ditch. Gates in the wall were wide enough for the baggage animals to enter and for the soldiers to dash out on quick raids if necessary. Inside the wall stood rows of tents, with the officers' quarters, a paymaster's office, and a hospital in the middle. Tents were always pitched in the same order so that the legionaries could find their quarters even in the dark. When the legionaries broke camp the next morning, they would pack up the tents and then burn the camp so the enemy could not use it.

After Augustus stationed the legions permanently in the empire's frontier areas, the camps became forts, complete with tall watch-towers set into their walls at regular intervals. Barracks replaced the tents, and the soldiers added clubrooms, a parade ground, workshops, warehouses, stables, markets, and baths. Some forts contained a temple and a sports arena as well. Gradually, towns grew up around the forts. Many of them—such as London, England; Vienna, Austria; and Bonn and Cologne, Germany—are major European cities today.

In addition to fighting, legionaries sometimes performed other functions. For example, they tracked down runaway slaves. Especially in the provinces, they served as a police force, patrolling streets, marketplaces, and harbor areas. They built bridges and roads. They transported official mail. And they protected government officials. Augustus created a personal bodyguard of soldiers called the Praetorian Guard. The Praetorians, who received more than three times the salary of the average legionary, escorted the emperor wherever he went.

Triumphal Parades

Except during much of Augustus's reign, war was a fairly commonplace event for the Romans. Because conquest brought them land, wealth, and power, the Romans honored successful generals with splendid parades called triumphs. (After 19 B.C.E., a general had to be a member of the imperial family in order to receive a triumph.)

A typical triumph lasted one to three days. At its head came the standards of the victorious legions, together with images of the Roman gods. These were followed by the spoils of war—wagons laden with captured arms that clanged against one another as they were borne along; baskets piled high with coins and jewels; herds of oxen and other animals; and finally the chained prisoners, condemned to death or lifelong slavery for having lost the war. Some triumphs also included floats, three or four stories high, that depicted scenes from the recent conflict: "a fertile land being ravaged . . . walls . . . being pounded down by siege-engines . . . men raising their hands in entreaty, firebrands being hurled at temples or buildings falling on their owners." The spectators could almost imagine that they were watching the actual scenes of war.

At last came the triumphant general, riding in a chariot drawn by four horses. His face was painted red to resemble the clay statue of Jupiter in Rome, and he wore special clothing of purple and gold, with a laurel wreath on his head. Next to him stood a servant who kept whispering in his ear, "Remember that you are mortal." It would not do for a general to get carried away just because one million Romans were cheering themselves hoarse in his honor! Behind the general marched senators and other government officials. And bringing up the rear tramped rank after rank of legionaries, reminding the people of the dangers they had overcome for the glory of Rome.

Public ceremonies in Rome took place in a huge open area called the Forum Romanum. The Forum also served as a political and social center where men campaigned for office and exchanged the latest news and gossip.

The Great Games

Even more spectacular than the triumphs were the public games that were held in Rome and other imperial cities. There were three kinds of games: gladiatorial fights between men, animal fights, and chariot races. The games were originally religious in nature, being held either as a funeral observance or to thank the gods for victory in battle. By the time of Augustus, they had become the empire's main form of entertainment.

The games were held in open-air buildings called amphitheaters. These contained a round or oval arena around which spectators sat on rows of benches. Government officials reserved the front rows for themselves, rich Romans took the next group of rows, and ordinary citizens filled up the rest. Peddlers moved up and down the connecting stairs selling cold drinks, sausages, and buns.

Gladiatorial fights took place in the afternoon, after business hours. The gladiators, mostly prisoners of war and criminals, trained in special schools. They did not use the javelins and swords of the legionaries. Instead, they fought with weapons that were as outlandish as possible. One gladiator might carry a curved dagger; another might be armed with a net and a three-pronged spear; a third might wear a helmet that came down over his eyes.

The games in Rome opened with the gladiators filing past the imperial box to greet the emperor: "Hail, Caesar. Those who are about to die salute you." After a few preliminary encounters with blunt weapons, the fights began in earnest, sometimes between a pair of gladiators, sometimes between teams of a dozen or more. One show featured 350 pairs of gladiators fighting at the same time. Flutes shrilled and trumpets blared as the combats continued. The crowd grew more and more excited as one fighter after another fell to the ground, his stomach torn open or his throat spurting blood. If he remained alive, he could ask the crowd for mercy by raising his left arm. If the spectators thought he had fought well, they put their thumbs down. If they wanted him killed, they gestured with thumbs up toward the breast. (Americans later reversed the signals—using thumbs-up for approval and thumbs-down for disapproval—because of a mistranslation.) Finally, the survivors withdrew to receive their gold and enjoy a few days more of life, while attendants dragged the corpses away and spread fresh sand over the blood-soaked arena in preparation for the next event.

Animal fights were held in the morning. Sometimes a lion was pitted against a gladiator. Sometimes a bear and a buffalo or two elephants were driven to fight each other. Sometimes archers went about dispatching a herd of ostriches or giraffes. As many as five thousand animals were often slaughtered in a single day, and hunters scoured the empire's provinces to round up fresh supplies. Demand ran so high that several species of animals—such as the Nubian hippopotamus, the North African elephant, and the Mesopotamian lion—were wiped out.

During the first century C.E., a remarkable event reportedly occurred at a beast show. An African slave named Androcles was sent into the arena with a lion. But the animal, instead of attacking Androcles, sat down on the ground. It turned out that back in Africa—according to the story—Androcles had removed a thorn from the lion's foot, and the animal remembered the man who had helped it. Androcles was freed and spent the rest of his life, accompanied by his lion on a leash, telling his story in taverns and receiving free drinks.

The Romans enjoyed chariot races almost as much as gladiatorial games and animal shows. Under the Republic, racehorses were

Gladiatorial fights continued until the fifth century C.E. Animal fights lasted until the sixth century C.E.

J.L. Gérome. Pinx

L. CHAPON. s

owned by wealthy individuals. Under the emperors, they were owned by groups of investors in four different stables—the Reds, the Whites, the Greens, and the Blues. Horses and drivers wore their stables' colors, and spectators placed bets accordingly. Emperors often backed a particular color, so Romans who disliked the emperor would bet against that color to show they were unhappy with his rule.

Racing chariots had two wheels and were pulled by teams of two or four horses. A driver either fastened the horses' reins to his belt or wrapped them around his waist. He also carried a knife with which to cut himself loose in case a wheel slipped off or the chariot pole broke as he careened along. Four teams at a time raced seven times around the track for a distance of about six miles. Attendants stood by to throw water on the chariots' smoking wheels. At first, ten to twelve races were held per day; later the number rose to twenty-four.

Romans often became very emotional about chariot races. People bet large sums of money on the outcome, while supporters of different colors fought bloody battles with one another in the streets. The emperor Caligula, who ruled from 37 C.E. to 41 C.E., had his troops patrol the neighborhood around his favorite racehorse's stable to make sure that no one disturbed the animal's rest the day before a race. Children played at racing in carts drawn by goats, sheep, dogs, and even geese.

Apartments and Houses

The only Romans who lived in single-family houses were the rich and those in rural areas. In Rome, most people lived in *insulae*, or "islands," multistoried wooden buildings that covered an entire block.

The typical island stood five or six stories high and was built around a courtyard. Occupying the ground floor were small shops that opened onto the street. Stairways led to the floors above. The landing on each floor contained two windows screened with wooden shutters against the wind and the rain. Rooms were windowless but sometimes had balconies. The higher the apartment, the cheaper the rent. Since most islands lacked both running water and latrines, tenants filled their water jugs at a street fountain and used chamber pots. They often emptied the pots from the windows on their floor instead of carrying them downstairs to a street drain. They lit candles made of tallow fat and used charcoal-burning braziers to keep warm during Rome's short but sharp winters.

Most islands were shoddily built, so they frequently collapsed into the streets. Fires were common. So were outbreaks of typhus and other diseases. Getting around was a problem, too. Only a few major streets had names and house numbers. Elsewhere, Romans were forced to orient themselves by a temple, a public

Many of Rome's buildings climbed the slopes of hills.

monument, or a city gate.

Individual Roman houses were in two main parts. In the front were the public rooms. The most important of these was the atrium, partly open to the sky, where the house's owner received visitors and attended to his business. Another important public room was the *tablinum*, which served as a library and also contained cabinets with wax masks of the owner's ancestors. In the back of the house were the private rooms—bedrooms, dining room, kitchen, and baths—arranged around an enclosed garden called a peristyle.

Public rooms were elaborately decorated, with marble floors, painted murals on the walls, inlaid tables, and candelabra made of silver and gold. The more luxurious the appointments, the greater the owner's prestige. Private rooms, on the other hand—except for the dining room—tended to be small and simply furnished. Bedrooms, for example, had just enough space for a wooden bed with a straw mattress and some woolen blankets, plus two or three chairs. There were no windows, and light came from lamps burning olive oil, which smoked and gave off an unpleasant odor.

The Romans had a passion for gardens. Wealthy individuals planted their peristyles with flowers, fruit trees, and evergreen shrubs. Roof gardens often contained fishponds. The very rich also surrounded their houses with gardens, which they filled with fountains, statues, and gorgeously colored peacocks. Even many *insulae* tenants kept window boxes and potted plants to remind them of nature.

In addition to pleasure gardens, well-to-do Romans owned vegetable gardens on the city's outskirts. There they grew a wide variety of staple foods, including greens, cucumbers, lettuces, and leeks; plants used for flavoring, such as garlic and onions; and medicinal herbs.

Farmhouses usually resembled traditional city houses, with private rooms in the rear and an atrium in front. However, the atrium of a farmhouse was really a courtyard, and the adjoining rooms served as stables, cowsheds, and outbuildings for farm equipment. Behind the house stood storage sheds for wheat, fruits, and wine. And nearby were the threshing floor, the manure pit, and the garden.

Food and Feasts

Many Romans did not eat breakfast. Those who did had a piece of bread, with perhaps some honey or dried fruit. Lunch usually consisted of cold leftovers from the night before, although city dwellers occasionally ordered sausages, fried fish, or salads at a local food stall or tavern. The most important meal of the day was dinner, which was served about four o'clock in the afternoon. If an individual was poor or was eating alone, the meal was simple: either bread or vegetables sprinkled with olive oil and washed down with a cup of watered wine. Many Romans, however, dined more elaborately with family and friends.

A full-fledged dinner consisted of three courses: the appetizer, the main course, and dessert. For everyday meals, the appetizer included a boiled egg, lettuce, and olives. The main course was wheatmeal porridge or vegetable soup, sometimes flavored with a ham bone. Dessert was apples and wine. Fish and pork were served on special occasions, such as a birthday or a marriage.

The menus for dinner parties given by rich Romans were much more elaborate. Appetizers included such exotic novelties as snails fed on milk, or grilled truffles in sausage skin. For the main course, a host might serve anything from peacock, roasted deer, or leg of boar to dormice stuffed with pork and pine kernels or lobster garnished with asparagus. Desserts ranged from wine cakes with honey to a fricassee of roses with pastry. Between the courses, diners often refreshed themselves with a bath and a massage, while singers, dancing girls, jugglers, clowns, acrobats, flutists, and lyre players provided entertainment. Occasionally a well-educated slave would read the work of a Greek author, or a host would recite his own poems. No wonder such banquets sometimes went on for as long as ten hours!

In this fresco, or wall painting, a Roman matron carries a plate of food.

Clothing

Roman clothing, like Roman furnishings, was simple. The most common fabrics were linen and wool. Although the Romans knew about Egyptian cotton, they used it mostly for ship awnings. Silk gradually became popular, but it was very expensive and considered to be rather daring since it was somewhat thin and transparent.

Both men and women wore a tunic, with or without sleeves, which they fastened with a belt. Men's tunics reached a little below the knees. Women's tunics fell to the ground and were often pleated. For dress-up occasions and political affairs, a man wore a toga over his tunic. A toga was basically a large blanket six yards long and two yards wide that was wrapped around the body so as to leave only the right hand free. The left hand held the toga's left tail in place. A woman wore a shawl over her tunic, pulling it up over her head when she went outdoors.

Clothing was almost uniformly white. Poor people's clothing, though, soon turned gray or brown since they could not afford to have it cleaned. The Romans bleached their clothing in urine, which contains ammonia, a cleaning chemical. Emperors, senators, and priests wore togas bordered with a purple stripe to distinguish them from other citizens. Brides were married in flame-colored veils. On their feet, Romans wore sandals at home and shoes that laced up the front if they were going out.

If the weather was very bad, the Romans wore waterproof cloaks made from wool that had not been cleaned or bleached and thus retained its natural oils. Men who worked outdoors, such as hunters and laborers, sometimes wore cloaks made of leather.

Men seldom wore jewelry, but wealthy women adorned their hands with as many gold rings as their fingers would hold. They pinned brooches on their shawls, stuck ornamental combs in their hair, and, if they were very rich, sported necklaces and bracelets of emeralds and pearls.

This gold and mother-of-pearl necklace dates from the first century B.C.E.

Roman clothing styles changed very little over the centuries

Beauty and Bathing

Most Roman men usually wore several days' growth of beard. Getting a shave was not a pleasant experience. Barbers in those days did not use soap but worked only with water and an iron razor. A few men had their bristles removed by tweezing, an equally uncomfortable process. All men wore their hair cropped short so as not to look like barbarians. Barbers used clumsy iron scissors that sometimes left a ragged cut. Younger men often had their barber style their hair with a curling iron so they would have ringlets on their foreheads. Older men dyed their hair when it began turning gray. Most men, especially city dwellers, perfumed it.

Poor Roman women did not fuss much with their hair. Well-to-do women, on the other hand, wore elaborate hairdos with braids, curls, twists, and bangs. Sometimes they added hairpieces to give their hair more body. Styles changed so frequently that it was hard to keep up. Fashionable women plucked their eyebrows and dyed their hair blond.

Both men and women tried to avoid baldness by smearing their scalps with various concoctions. Marrow from deer bones was highly recommended, as was fat from such animals as bears and sheep. If these remedies did not work, balding Romans wore wigs.

Roman women used makeup lavishly. They painted their faces with chalk or white lead, rouged their lips and cheeks with red ocher, and darkened their eyebrows with charcoal or a paste made

Fashionable Roman women liked to change their hairstyles frequently. They liked to wear makeup, too, which they removed only at bedtime.

from crushed ants' eggs.

Although most Romans lived in what we would consider unsanitary conditions, they kept themselves very clean personally. Both men and women bathed every day, usually in the afternoon at a public bath. The baths were huge structures, able to accommodate as many as three thousand bathers at a time. They were magnificent as well. The walls were often made of marble and the floors were covered with ornamental tiles, while the ceilings soared one hundred feet into the air. Usually there was one set of rooms for men and another for women. If there were no separate rooms, women usually bathed in the morning and men in the afternoon. The admission price was low enough even for poor Romans, and sometimes an emperor or a wealthy person would agree to pay everyone's fees for anything from a day to a year.

Bathers usually started out by wrestling, playing ball, or sunbathing in order to warm up their bodies. They then spent time

Many Roman women woke bikinis and exercised with weights and balls, just as women do today.

sweating in the steam room and cooling down in the warm-air room. The next step was the cold room, where they scraped their bodies with a curved blade made of metal, bone, or wood and then plunged into a cold swimming pool. After that—if they could afford it—they had masseurs rub them down with oil and splash them with perfume. If they wanted to, they could read books in the library, stroll through the garden, buy sausages and other snacks from vendors, or talk with friends before going on their way.

The Family Circle

The Roman family was headed by the paterfamilias, the leading male. It included his wife, his children, dependent relatives, and slaves. Sons were valued more than daughters. If a man had no son, he would adopt a relative, as when Julius Caesar adopted Octavian and Augustus adopted Tiberius.

In theory, the power of the paterfamilias over his family was absolute. He could divorce his wife at will, abandon an unwanted infant on a garbage dump, sell his children into slavery, collect his sons' wages, and even kill a family member to protect the family's honor. In practice, however, the typical paterfamilias was quite lenient. He usually consulted with all adult family males before selling property, arranging a marriage, or making other important decisions. And while he seldom showed affection in public, he often revealed his true feelings on tombstone inscriptions such as this one: "My wife, who died before me . . . my one and only, a loving woman who possessed my heart, she lived as a faithful wife to a faithful husband with affection equal to my own."

Although Roman women were considered citizens, they did not have the right to vote or to hold public office. However, they could attend the theater and shop in the public marketplace. Most important of all, they could inherit property. And although a male relative was supposed to manage it, in reality a woman who owned property usually looked after it herself. Many middle-class and poor women worked at various professions and trades. They were doctors, midwives, fishmongers, laundresses, textile workers, and maids.

Marriages were considered to be made between families rather than individuals. They were meant to improve a family's political position or increase its wealth. Girls married after they reached the age of twelve, while boys married after they reached the age of fourteen. Most Romans stayed married all their lives, but divorce was common among the upper class.

Getting an Education

Roman boys were taught how to read and write by their fathers. When they reached the age of seven, rich boys frequently were tutored at home, usually by an educated Greek slave. Otherwise, boys went to school. However, education was not compulsory. Also, it was supported by fees rather than taxes. So poor boys and farmers' sons often grew up illiterate.

There were no school buildings in Rome in those days. A teacher would hold classes on a rooftop or rent a room in a ground-floor shop, where noises from the street made discipline a problem. Teachers often kept order by hitting students on the hand with a cane or flogging them with a leather whip. The school day was fairly long: six hours with a noon recess for lunch. On the other hand, frequent holidays and a long summer vacation meant the school year was rather short. Fees were low, and many teachers lived hand-to-mouth.

The main subjects were the three Rs. Reading and writing Latin was easy, but the Roman numeral system made arithmetic cumbersome. The Romans used combinations of seven letters for their numerals: I (1), V (5), X (10), L (50), C (100), D (500), and M (1,000). Thus, where we write 78, the Romans wrote LXXVIII. Students used a pointed iron pen called a stylus to scratch their letters on a waxed wooden writing tablet.

When they reached the age of twelve, boys began the study of literature and Greek. Learning Greek was important, not only because so many great books were written in Greek but also because it was the common language of the eastern Mediterranean. After boys turned seventeen, they entered the army or, if they were aristocrats, studied philosophy and public speaking to prepare for a government career.

Roman girls learned how to read and write either in school or from a tutor at home. Their mothers often taught them how to spin and weave.

Slavery

Of all ancient civilizations, Rome was the one that depended the most on slave labor. Slavery had always existed. But it really started to expand during the second century B.C.E., when Rome's conquests spread around the Mediterranean and hordes of captives began pouring into the city. (Unlike slavery in the United States, slavery in Rome had nothing to do with the color of a person's skin.) By the time of Augustus, there was one slave for every two or three Roman citizens, or about 400,000 slaves for the city's population of one million.

Poor people did not own any slaves. Even lower-middle-class families, however, usually had three to eight slaves in their households. Rich Romans might have a thousand slaves, while some emperors boasted as many as 20,000. Slaves were barbers and valets, cooks and bakers, cleaners and gardeners, doormen and waiters, ladies' maids and dressmakers. Children were brought up by slave nurses. When rich ladies went visiting or shopping, they rode in a litter carried by six to eight slaves. A wealthy man who ventured outdoors at night was accompanied by a bodyguard of slaves as protection against thieves and bullies.

The price of slaves varied. It fell after a successful military campaign, when the market became glutted, and rose if the slave was particularly good-looking or had a special skill. Educated Greeks were especially prized as tutors, doctors, librarians, and artists. If a

A slave holds a goblet in this ancient Roman stone carving. Slaves were gradually freed in Rome, but only because it became more costly to keep a slave than it did to hire a free person.

slave knew how to keep accounts or make jewelry, his master would often hire him out or set him up in business. The slave could keep part of his fee, save up his money, and eventually buy his freedom.

Many slaves were employed in working for the city. They built roads, bridges, and other public structures. They served as attendants in the temples. They repaired the aqueducts that provided a plentiful water supply of forty gallons a day for every inhabitant. Except at the very top, Augustus's administrative staff consisted entirely of slaves and freedmen. They kept in constant touch with army commanders and provincial governors and supervised the mint, the post, tax collection, and the distribution of free wheat. Less fortunate slaves were put to work in the city's mines or on its ships, where they lasted perhaps one to two years before dying from exhaustion.

In early years, many Romans treated their slaves brutally, beating them and even killing them by crucifixion. Many slaves ran away from their masters. In 73 B.C.E., a gladiator named Spartacus led a revolt of some 90,000 slaves. The men terrorized the Roman countryside for almost two years before being defeated in battle. In 63 B.C.E., an ambitious politician named Catiline promised freedom to any slaves who would fight for him in his attempt to gain political control of Rome.

By the time of Augustus, laws were being passed to improve the treatment of slaves. For example, the fourth emperor, Claudius I, who reigned from 41 C.E. to 54 C.E., prohibited slave owners from killing or abandoning slaves who fell ill and could not work. By then, too, many Romans were freeing their slaves and even leaving them money in their wills. Historians estimate that by the second century C.E., eight out of ten of Rome's inhabitants had at least one slave ancestor.

Religion

There were two kinds of religion in Rome. One was the private religion led by the paterfamilias within the home. The other was the public religion, which was carried on by priests who were elected by the citizens.

Family gods were known as lares and penates. The lares protected the family's house and farmland. People placed bronze statuettes of the lares on their tables when they sat down to eat. The penates guarded the family's storehouse. People burned candles, incense, or bits of food before statuettes of the penates.

The most important public gods were Jupiter, god of the sky and father of the Roman state, and Mars, god of war and seedtime. (Planting seeds and warfare went together because the early Romans used to fight their neighbors for new farmland in the spring.) They and other gods and goddesses were thought to live in temples, where they were represented by painted marble statues. Romans who worshipped a particular god or goddess would simply drop into the proper temple and turn up their palms in prayer before the statue. In addition to paying an admission fee, they usually made an offering of money or livestock.

The temples were not just places of worship. They served as banks where Romans deposited their gold and silver. They served as art museums, where Romans displayed sculptures and other art objects captured in battle. Sometimes they even served as meeting

This maenad is a follower of the Greek god Dionysus, who gave humankind wine and drama. The Romans believed that maenads lived in forests or on mountains, where they worshipped Dionysus with wild dancing.

places for the Senate.

The Roman calendar was filled with religious festivals. For example, on March 1, the start of the Roman year, six young women known as Vestal Virgins relit the city's sacred hearth fire. In September, the Romans held games in honor of Jupiter. And from December 17 to December 20, they celebrated the Saturnalia. Everyone joined in. Schools and law courts were closed, and even the slave markets were shut down. The holiday began with a public sacrifice in honor of Saturn, the harvest god, followed by a public feast. Then the Romans, wearing red pointed caps and colored costumes, paraded through the city's streets, throwing wheat and barley in all directions and singing at the top of their lungs. Houses were trimmed with evergreens, and gifts for family and friends were chosen and wrapped in preparation for the private dinners that were held on the second day. Everyone ate roast young pig. And tables were turned as masters waited on their household slaves.

Roman emperors capitalized on the people's religious feelings by acting as the state's *pontifex maximus*, or "chief priest." They also had themselves worshipped as gods. Conquered peoples showed they were loyal to Rome by burning incense before a statue of the emperor.

In addition to worshipping their gods and goddesses, the Romans were anxious to determine the future. Fortune-telling was popular. Even Octavian consulted an astrologer when he was eighteen. According to the story, the astrologer had no sooner looked at his charts than he threw himself at Octavian's feet as if the youth were an Asian king.

The Romans also looked for signs from the gods before making major political decisions or going to war. They called this "taking the auspices," or foretelling from the flight of birds. For example, according to legend, Romulus and his twin brother, Remus, both wanted to lay out the settlement of Rome. So they agreed to watch the flight of vultures. Remus spotted six. Romulus, who was looking in a different direction, saw twelve—and thus became the city's founder. Legions and warships were accompanied by a special officer with a coop of sacred chickens. If the chickens gobbled up their food before a battle, it meant the Romans would win. Once an admiral, angry that his chickens refused to eat, threw them overboard, exclaiming, "If they won't eat, let them drink!" He lost the battle and, when he returned to Rome, was put on trial and fined heavily. It served him right for ignoring a message from the gods!

As the years went on, the Romans imported religions from the lands they fought against or conquered. From Egypt came the worship of Isis, the goddess of marriage and childbirth. In paintings and statues, she was usually shown with the infant Horus in her arms. She was married to Osiris, who died and was reborn. From Persia came Mithraism, a religion that was extremely popular among the legionaries. (Women could not take part in its rituals.) Mithraism taught that life was a struggle between the forces of good and those of evil. It also taught that the soul lived forever and that Mithra, a sun god whose birthday was December 25, would help his baptized followers enter heaven after they died. From Palestine came Judaism, with its belief in a god of justice and a society in which everyone was treated fairly. And within a few years after Augustus's death, there came another religion from Palestine: Christianity. By the end of the fourth century C.E., it had become the only official religion of Rome.

PART THREE

Bands of musicians often wandered through Rome's streets playing such instruments as the harp and the bronze horn.

Their Own Words

Ancient Romans, like people today, were often worried about a sick or injured relative. Advice for cures was a bit different back then, however. A fond brother by the name of Cassius Octavius (59 C.E.–125 C.E.) wrote the following letter to his sister Julia:

I have been extremely worried ever since I got your letter telling me that you were bitten by a spider hidden among vegetables from the garden. Do you know what kind of spider it was? In Apulia . . . there are a lot of dangerous spiders called tarantulas. Or could it be one of those phalangia *Pliny writes about?—This seems more likely, since they are to be found among vegetables. The best remedy for the fever and dizziness which result from their bites is—as you probably know—to crush the body of the spider on the wound, or if that's impossible, cover the place with a piece of its web. Although you tell me you are now better, I am still concerned about you, for Pliny says that a spider bite can also make a woman barren [unable to have children]. So I advise you to come to Rome as soon as you can, and we will go together to make a sacrifice at the temple of the Great Mother [Cybele], the Eastern goddess who is famous for bestowing fertility.*

People two thousand years ago used to say, "All roads lead to Rome." And in fact, Rome's road system was probably the most extensive in the world. Still, travel on land and sea could be quite an adventure. The poet Horace wrote an account of a journey he made in 38 B.C.E. He started out on the famous Appian Way, which ran some 360 miles from Rome southeast to Brindisi, in the heel of the Italian "boot":

I left lofty Rome on a trip, stopping first at Aricia,
At a quiet little inn. . . . From Aricia
We pushed on to Forum Appi, a place jammed with boatmen
And sharp innkeepers. This forty miles took us two days—

Roman roads were built in straight lines wherever possible. Each mile was marked off by a round milestone, and there were post stations and resthouses for messengers and government officials at regular intervals. Some Roman roads, like the Appian Way, are still in use today, more than 2,200 years after they were built.

Took us slowpokes two days; real travelers make it in one.
The Appian Way is less rough if you take it in stages.
At Forum Appi I found the water so foul
I made war on my stomach and waited fuming while friends
Finished their dinner.
    Now night was preparing to spread
Her darkness on earth, to station her stars in the heavens.
And boatmen and slaves began cursing each other to pieces.
"In here with that sieve!" yells a porter. "OH, NO!" shouts a slave,
"You've already got three hundred on board! Call it quits!"
Never take a night boat, reader. You spend the first hour
Paying fares and hitching up the mule. Then fearless mosquitoes
And resonant swamp frogs keep sleep safely at bay.
A sailor and passenger, soused with cheap wine, compete
In songs to their absent girl friends. The mule driver finally
Drops off to sleep: the lazy driver lets the mule browse,
Fastens the rope to a rock, stretches out, and snores.
    Dawn was already at hand before we observed
That the boat hadn't budged an inch. Then a hot-tempered tourist
Leaped ashore, cut a switch from a willow, lit into the mule
And the driver, drumming on their domes and their bones.
Even so, it was ten when we finally got through the canal.

Under the Roman Republic, plaintiffs and defendants used
to plead their own cases in court before a panel of fifty to sixty
aristocrats. By the time of Augustus, a professional class of lawyers
had developed. Usually the more flowery and spellbinding his
speech on behalf of a client, the more successful a lawyer was,
even if some of the things he spoke about had nothing to do
with the case at hand. The poet Martial, who lived from 40 C.E. to
104 C.E., took one such lawyer to task in a poem:

Mine's not a lurid criminal case,
Or anything of that sort.
I claim my neighbor stole three goats;
That's all you need prove in court.
So why these learned anecdotes,
About Caesar, Pompeii, Hannibal?
Get on to those three goats!

Martial did not limit his critical comments to lawyers. He did not think much of doctors, either:

I had a cold. The doctor came
*   And five assistants, too.*
They laid ten icy hands on me,
*   And now I've got the flu.*

While Martial poked fun at Roman society, other poets wrote about love. Ovid, who lived from 43 B.C.E. to 18 C.E., described the plight of a young man in love with two girls at once:

You used to tell me, Graecinus—
yes, you were the one, I am sure, I remember each word—
that a man may love two girls at the same time.
You tricked me into it.
It's all your fault I was caught unarmed and napping.
Look, to my shame, I'm mad about
two girls at the same moment.

Both are delightful.
Both spend much time and trouble on their clothes,
and which knows more than the other is hard to say.
The first's more beautiful than the second,
the second's more beautiful than the first.

The first pleases me more than the second,
the second pleases me more than the first.
My passions eddy to and fro.
I'm like a skiff sent helterskelter by a changeable wind.
I'm most distracted.
Why, Venus, keep on doubling my despairs?
Wasn't one piece enough to break my heart?

The dilemma of the young man in the poem is reflected in this floor decoration showing a man and two women at a banquet. The slave in the background is playing the panpipes.

Running for public office during the Roman Republic bore a great resemblance to running for public office in the United States today. Each year, the Romans chose two consuls to serve as chief executives and to lead the army in battle. When Marcus Tullius

Cicero ran for consul in 64 B.C.E., his brother Quintus sent him a letter instructing him how to behave:

> *Take care to have followers at your heels daily, of every kind, class, and age; because from their number people can figure out how much power and support you are going to have at the polls. . . . You particularly need to use flattery. No matter how vicious and vile it is on the other days of a man's life, when he runs for office it is [absolutely necessary]. . . .*
>
> *[Getting votes] requires calling everyone by his name. . . . make it clear you know people's names. . . . practice, get better at it day to day. . . .*
>
> *If you make a promise, the matter is not fixed, it's for a future day . . . but, if you say no, you are sure to [turn off] people right away.*

Candidates for office gave speeches appealing to citizens to vote for them. The following speech was delivered in 107 B.C.E. by Gaius Marius in his campaign for the consulship. Marius was an able general who had won major victories in Africa and Gaul. However, he was a so-called "new man," one whose ancestors had never held office in the Roman government. As a result, in spite of his military accomplishments, established senatorial families were horrified at the idea that he might be elected:

> *Compare me, the "new man," my fellow citizens, with those proud nobles. What they know from lectures and books I have*

myself seen, myself done. What they learn from handbooks I know from service. They despise me for an upstart, I despise their worthlessness. . . . My own belief is that men are born equal and alike: nobility is achieved by bravery. . . .

My expressions are not elegant; I don't care. . . . I never learned Greek; I never wanted to, for Greek did little for the character of its professors. I did learn things far more useful to the state—to strike the enemy, to be vigilant on guard, to fear nothing except disgrace, to endure heat and cold alike, to sleep on the ground, to bear privation and fatigue at the same time. . . . They say I am vulgar and unmannerly because I cannot give a dainty dinner, that I have no entertainer or cook that costs more than a farm steward. I am happy to admit the charge, fellow citizens. From my father and other righteous men I learned that daintiness is appropriate to women, strenuousness to men, that good men ought to have more glory than riches, that weapons, not furniture is the true ornament.

During election campaigns, supporters and opponents of candidates often scrawled their opinions on walls that faced the street. (The high cost of writing materials made posters too expensive.) The following graffiti were painted on walls at Pompeii about 80 B.C.E.:

1. Numerius Barcha, a fine man; I appeal to you to elect him member of the Board of Duoviri [the equivalent of mayors]. So may Venus of Pompeii, holy, hallowed goddess, be kind to you.
2. Numerius Veius Barcha, may you rot!
3. The muleteers ask for Gaius Julius Polybius as a member of the Board of Duoviri.
4. I appeal to you to elect Gaius Julius Polybius. . . ; he makes good bread.

In 79 C.E., almost 160 years after these elections were held in Pompeii, the city was destroyed by one of the greatest volcanic eruptions in history. Pliny the Younger, who was a few miles from

The thirty-foot layer of ash that covered Pompeii after the eruption of Mount Vesuvius preserved most of the small seaside town. Since its site was discovered in 1748, excavations have revealed all sorts of details about the lives of its inhabitants. Finds have included furniture, graffiti, and even carbonized loaves of bread.

the scene when Mount Vesuvius erupted, described the event and the resulting death of his uncle in a letter:

My uncle [Pliny the Elder] was stationed at Misenum [at the western tip of the Bay of Naples, about twenty miles from Mount Vesuvius] in active command of the fleet. On 24 August, in the early afternoon, my mother drew his attention to a cloud of unusual size and appearance. . . . He . . . climbed up to a place which would give him the best view. . . . [The cloud's] general appearance can best be expressed as being like an umbrella pine, for it rose to a great height on a sort of trunk and then split off into branches. . . . In places it looked white, elsewhere blotched and dirty, according to the amount of soil and ashes it carried with it. My uncle's scholarly . . . [judgment] saw at once that it was important enough for a closer inspection, and he ordered a boat to be made ready. . . .

As he was leaving the house he was handed a message from Rectina, wife of Tascus whose house was at the foot of the mountain. . . . She was terrified by the danger threatening her and implored him to rescue her from her fate. He changed his plans, and what he had begun in a spirit of inquiry he completed as a hero. He gave orders for the warships to be launched and went on board himself with the intention of bringing help to many more people besides Rectina, for this lovely stretch of coast was thickly populated. He hurried to the place which everyone else was hastily leaving, steering his course straight for the danger zone. He was entirely fearless, describing each new movement and phase of the . . . [eruption] to be noted down exactly as he observed them. Ashes were already falling, hotter and thicker as the ships drew near, followed by bits of pumice [a light form of solidified lava] and blackened stones, charred and cracked by the flames: then suddenly they were in shallow water, and the shore was blocked by the debris from the mountain. For a moment my uncle wondered whether to turn back, but when the helmsman advised this he refused, telling him that Fortune stood by the courageous and they must make for [the home of] Pomponianus [a friend] at Stabiae [four miles south of Pompeii]. . . .

They [Pliny, Pomponianus, and the rest of the household] debated whether to stay indoors or take their chance in the open, for the buildings were now shaking with violent shocks, and seemed to be swaying to and fro as if they were torn from their foundations. Outside on the other hand, there was the danger of falling pumice-stones. . . . however, after comparing the risks they chose the latter. . . . As a protection against falling objects they put pillows on their heads tied down with clothes. . . .

My uncle decided to go down to the shore and investigate . . . the possibility of any escape by sea, but he found the waves still wild and dangerous. A sheet was spread on the ground for him to lie down, and he repeatedly asked for cold water to drink. Then the flames and smell of sulphur which gave warning of the approaching fire drove the others to take flight and roused him to stand up. He stood leaning on two slaves and then suddenly collapsed, I imagine because the dense fumes choked his breathing by blocking his windpipe. . . . When daylight returned on the 26th—two days after the last day he had seen—his body was found intact and uninjured, still fully clothed and looking more like sleep than death.

For Further Reading

Brooks, P. S., and N. Z. Walworth. *When the World Was Rome.* Philadelphia: Lippincott, 1972.

Burrell, Roy. *The Romans.* New York: Oxford University Press, 1991.

Casson, Lionel. *Everyday Life in Ancient Rome.* Baltimore: Johns Hopkins University Press, 1998.

Duggan, Alfred. *The Romans.* Cleveland and New York: World Publishing Company, 1964.

Hinds, Kathryn. *The Ancient Romans.* New York: Marshall Cavendish, 1997.

James, Simon. *Ancient Rome.* New York: Alfred A. Knopf, 1990.

MacDonald, Fiona. *A Roman Fort.* New York: Peter Bedrick Books, 1993.

Miquel, Pierre. *Life in Ancient Rome.* Morristown, NJ: Silver Burdett Company, 1981.

Nardo, Don. *The Age of Augustus.* San Diego: Lucent Books, 1997.

————. *The Battle of Actium.* San Diego: Lucent Books, 1996.

————. *Life in Ancient Rome.* San Diego: Lucent Books, 1996.

Walworth, Nancy Zinsser. *Augustus Caesar.* New York: Chelsea House, 1989.

Windrow, Martin. *The Roman Legionary.* New York: Franklin Watts, 1984.

ON-LINE INFORMATION*

http://www.pbs.org/mpt/augustus/resources/main/html/pages
> Rome at the time of Augustus. There are good links on this website.

http://www.julen.net/ancient/index.html
> An excellent index to resources on the time of Augustus.

*Websites change from time to time. For additional on-line information, check with the media specialist at your local library.

Bibliography

Balsdon, J. P. V. D. *Life and Leisure in Ancient Rome.* New York: McGraw-Hill, 1969.

Bernard, Leon, and Theodore B. Hodges, eds. *Readings in European History.* New York: Macmillan Company, n. d.

Bingham, Marjorie Wall, and Susan Hill Gross. *Women in Ancient Greece and Rome.* St. Louis Park, MN: Glenhurst Publications, 1983.

Bovie, Smith Palmer. *The Satires and Epistles of Horace.* Chicago: University of Chicago Press, n. d.

Casson, Lionel. "... Politics As Usual in Ancient Rome." *Smithsonian,* October 1984.

———. "... a Time without Any Lawyers at All." *Smithsonian,* October 1987.

———. "... If You Sent Me 200 Drachmas." *Smithsonian,* April 1983.

———, ed. *Classical Age.* New York: Dell Publishing, 1965.

Cowell, F. R. *Everyday Life in Ancient Rome.* New York: G. P. Putnam's Sons, 1961.

Dupont, Florence. *Daily Life in Ancient Rome.* Cambridge, MA: Blackwell, 1993.

Foster, Genevieve. *Augustus Caesar's World.* New York: Charles Scribner's Sons, 1947.

Grant, Michael. *The Twelve Caesars.* New York: Charles Scribner's Sons, 1975.

———, ed. *Readings in the Classical Historians.* New York: Charles Scribner's Sons, 1992.

Hadas, Moses. *A History of Rome.* Garden City, NY: Doubleday & Co., 1956.

———. *Imperial Rome.* New York: Time-Life Books, 1965.

———. *The Stoic Philosophy of Seneca.* Garden City, NY: Doubleday & Co., 1958.

Le Bohec, Yann. *The Imperial Roman Army.* New York: Hippocrene Books, 1994.

Lefkowitz, Mary R., and Maureen B. Fant. *Women's Life in Greece and Rome.* Baltimore: Johns Hopkins University Press, 1982.

Lindsay, Jack, ed. and trans. *Ribaldry of Ancient Rome: An Intimate Portrait of Romans in Love.* New York: Frederick Ungar Publishing, 1961.

Liversidge, Joan. *Everyday Life in the Roman Empire.* New York: G. P. Putnam's Sons, 1975.

Massie, Allan. *The Caesars.* New York: Franklin Watts, 1984.

Miquel, Pierre. *Life in Ancient Rome.* Morristown, NJ: Silver Burdett Company, 1981.

Nardo, Don. *The Age of Augustus.* San Diego: Lucent Books, 1997.

Payne, Robert. *Ancient Rome.* New York: American Heritage Press, 1970.

Radice, Betty. *The Letters of the Younger Pliny.* Baltimore: Penguin Books, 1963.

Starr, Chester G. *The Roman Empire, 27 B.C.–A.D. 476: A Study in Survival.* New York: Oxford University Press, 1982.

Syme, Ronald. *The Roman Revolution.* Oxford: Oxford University Press, 1963.

Tingay, G. I. F., and J. Badcock. *These Were the Romans.* 2d ed. Chester Springs, PA: Dufour Editions, 1989.

Wills, Garry, ed. *Roman Culture: Weapons and the Man.* New York: George Braziller, 1966.

Winer, Bart. *Life in the Ancient World.* New York: Random House, 1961.

Workman, B. K. *They Saw It Happen in Classical Times.* Oxford: Basil Blackwell, 1964.

Notes

Part One: The Most Remarkable Roman

Page 13 "The young man": Payne, *Ancient Rome*, p. 157.
Page 17 "I refused every office": Hadas, *Imperial Rome*, p. 73.
Page 18 "clothed in marble": Nardo, *The Age of Augustus*, p. 42.
Page 19 "Remember, Roman": Payne, *Ancient Rome*, p. 77.
Page 22 "O—what shall I call you?": Bernard and Hodges, *Readings in European History*, p. 23.
Page 22 "I could not bear": Payne, *Ancient Rome*, p. 164.
Page 25 "How have I played my part": Massie, *The Caesars*, p. 83.
Page 25 "Farewell, Livia": Massie, *The Caesars*, p. 83.

Part Two: Everyday Life in Imperial Rome

Page 33 "a fertile land being ravaged": Workman, *They Saw It Happen in Classical Times*, p. 158.
Page 33 "Remember that you are mortal": Tingay and Badcock, *These Were the Romans*, p. 89.
Page 35 "Hail, Caesar": Cowell, *Everyday Life in Ancient Rome*, p. 174, and Hadas, *Imperial Rome*, p. 50.
Page 49 "My wife, who died before me": Lefkowitz and Fant, *Women's Life in Greece and Rome*, p. 134.
Page 59 "If they won't eat": Dupont, *Daily Life in Ancient Rome*, p. 183.

Part Three: The Romans in Their Own Words

Page 62 "I have been extremely worried": Miquel, *Life in Ancient Rome*, p. 58.
Page 63 "I left lofty Rome": Bovie, *The Satires and Epistles of Horace*, pp. 58–59.
Page 65 "Mine's not a lurid criminal case": Casson, "Imagine, If You Will, a Time without Any Lawyers at All," p. 128.
Page 65 "I had a cold": Casson, *Classical Age*, p. 576.
Page 65 "You used to tell me": Lindsay, *Ribaldry of Ancient Rome*, pp. 102–103.
Page 67 "Take care to have followers": Casson, "And Never Say No," p. 131.
Page 67 "Compare me": Hadas, *A History of Rome*, pp. 52–53.
Page 68 "Numerius Barcha": Workman, *They Saw It Happen in Classical Times*, p. 88.
Page 70 "My uncle": Radice, *The Letters of the Younger Pliny*, pp. 166–168.
Page 72 "On receiving this letter": Casson, "It Would Be Very Nice If You Sent Me 200 Drachmas," pp. 125–126.
Page 73 "A man is a fool": Hadas, *The Stoic Philosophy of Seneca*, pp. 194, 214.
Page 73 "Physical characteristics": Grant, *Readings in the Classical Historians*, p. 515.

Index

Page numbers for illustrations are in boldface.